BIRTHDAY MONTH BLESSINGS BOOK

Bob Perry, Amy Lykosh

MAKARIOS
PRESS

CONTENTS

INTRODUCTION

I have, at times, asked Bob to pray a prayer or a blessing, thinking he will simply open his mouth and pray.

He always surprises me, though, because first he pauses, listening and asking, coming before the Lord. He waits until he hears.

Each of these blessings is built on a scripture that the Lord brought to mind as Bob listened. He then prayed a blessing out of that passage, creating this collection of blessings to meet our most important needs and desires, not only as individuals, but also as part of a family and a community.

Timeless, precious blessings.

He originally prayed these as a series around a birthday month.

We love the idea, not just of celebrating a birthday, but of celebrating each person all month.

A healthy form of self-care, celebrating the goodness of God in creating each one of us.

You can use this book in many ways.

Born in January? Start with Day 1 on January 1 and read through January 31.

Or, if born on January 15, start with Day 1 on January 15 and read through February 15.

Or start whenever you want, skip days when needed, and read more than one if you're hungry for more.

However you read: you are celebrated and blessed.

Happy Birthday Month! May the beauty and favor of the Lord our God rest on you!

We celebrate with you!

You are royally blessed and highly favored!

1

DAY 1

ISAIAH 41:10

S *o do not fear, for I am with you; do not be dismayed, for I am your God. I will strengthen you and help you; I will uphold you with my righteous right hand.*

Thank you that you are our Lord, our God. You take us by the hand. You say to us: "Do not fear, for I am with you."

The scriptures say over and over again, "Fear not. Do not be afraid. Do not fear, for I am with you. Do not be dismayed."

Lord, we thank you for your Divine Presence. We thank you for the encouragement that you give us that the divine helper is here.

The supernatural, divine hand of God is upon us. Supernatural, divine care. And the strength of God.

Lord, we seek your face. Your face is what we want. And I proclaim over us: do not fear anything, for the Lord you God is with us. Do not be afraid, for our God is with us. He will strengthen us.

He wants us to know that we can be assured that he will help us. We can certainly know that he will take hold of us with his righteous right hand, his hand of justice, of power, of victory, of salvation.

For the Lord our God holds us. He says, "Do not fear, child of God. Do not worry. Do not be afraid. Do not be dismayed."

While we are on the journey, and we want to get to the destination the Lord has for us, he will strengthen us. He is strengthening us.

He strengthens us, and he holds us.

He strengthens us, and he empowers us.

He says, "Don't panic. I'm with you. Don't panic, child. I'm with you."

We have no need to fear, for our God is with us. No need to worry about our strength or energy. God is giving us strength. He will help us.

And there's no need to worry about our direction, because he's going to keep us steady. He has a firm grip on our life and our calling.

Lord, thank you that we are fearing not, for you are with us.

We don't have to be dismayed or discouraged, for you are our God, and you're strengthening us, you're energizing us. You're giving us fresh new vision.

We speak this blessing on the first day of the birthday month of refreshing: a bit of energy. And every day, a promise in the scriptures. For the Lord says, "Fear not, for I am with you."

Thank you, Lord.

Now bless us with clear revelation that angels are part of the divine help, and that the Lord is with us, and the Spirit of God is with us, and the presence of the Lord.

Thank you for your supernatural help.

Lord, thank you that you are our guide. You quiet the enemies, and you strengthen us.

Bless this month of prayer. Amen.

2

DAY 2

II Timothy 4:7

I *have fought the good fight, I have finished the race, I have kept the faith.*

Paul wrote this to his spiritual son Timothy.

Lord, thank you for Paul's powerful testimony, reminded us that we are in spiritual warfare. We face a battle. We face a fight.

And we are in a Christian race. We are running a marathon.

Lord, you give us your power to fight the good fight of faith.

Lord, thank you that we are children of God, children after your heart. We are staying on course.

Lord, we think about runners, and how they finish the race.

Like those runners, let us keep believing. Let us keep pushing ahead, let us keep trusting God, let us keep working.

Father, you shout applause for us. You cheer us on. You encourage us to continue to run hard, to finish, to believe all the way to the finish that the Lord our God is with us.

Lord, let us continue to persevere, for the Lord our God is with us.

Like Paul told Timothy: finish the course, fight the good fight of faith, keep the faith.

Child of God, you have fought well in the past.

You are running well, you are pursuing well in the presence. You are a person of excellence.

You will finish the race. You will keep the faith.

For you are fighting this noble fight with integrity and character. You are a person of conquest, completing the purpose and call on your life.

You are firmly guarding the gospel. You are firmly grounded in faith.

You walk with him, and you trust him.

Lord, we thank you that we are not running aimlessly. We are not air-boxing, fighting to beat the air. No. We are focused. We are children with your call, with your passion and with your purpose.

Lord, thank you for the ways you have trained us and disciplined us.

Thank you for the ways we have been faithful. And thank you for the ways that we haven't been faithful, that you are ever the faithful one.

Bless us indeed, Lord, for walking in your ways. Bless us with courage and strength. Bless us with perseverance and endurance. Give us strength, Lord. Give us courage.

And help us, Lord, as we walk in your ways. In Jesus' name, amen.

3

DAY 3

EPHESIANS 3:16-21

I pray that out of his glorious riches he may strengthen you with power through his Spirit in your inner being, so that Christ may dwell in your hearts through faith. And I pray that you, being rooted and established in love, may have power, together with all the Lord's holy people, to grasp how wide and long and high and deep is the love of Christ, and to know this love that surpasses knowledge—that you may be filled to the measure of all the fullness of God.

Now to him who is able to do immeasurably more than all we ask or imagine, according to his power that is at work within us, to him be glory in the church and in Christ Jesus throughout all generations, for ever and ever! Amen.

As 150 leaders gathered to pray, they asked Papa Don Finto, 93 years young, to pray.

He said, "You can't ever go wrong with praying an apostolic prayer as a blessing."

Father, may you bless us out of your honorable and glorious riches. May you strengthen us in the spirit. May you fill our souls with the power of the Holy Spirit.

Lord, through faith in the anointed one, Jesus, may the love of Christ find rich soil in our hearts.

Lord, with all the people of God, the saints around the world and throughout history, we understand the love of the anointed one is infinitely long, infinitely wide, infinitely high, and infinitely deep, surpassing any previous experience and any knowledge and understanding.

God, may your fullness flood us this year, with a greater anointing and a greater blessing.

I speak this doxology of praise over us: to the God who can do many awe-inspiring things, immeasurable things, things greater than we ever could ask or imagine, through the power at work in us, to him be all the glory. To Christ, to Jesus the Anointed One, from this generation to the next, forever and ever.

May he bless the work of our hands.

May the Father of glory strengthen you in your inner being, revealing more of his love, more of his anointing, and more of his grace.

And may he do more in you than what you could ask, think, or even imagine.

Lord, do great things for us. In Jesus' name. Amen.

4

DAY 4

PSALM 118:24

This is the day that the LORD has made; let us rejoice and be glad in it.[1]

Father, thank you for the blessing of the Lord upon us.

As *The Voice* says: "This is the day the Eternal God has made; let us celebrate and be happy today."

Lord, we worship you. We celebrate your goodness and your presence. We acknowledge again the power of rejoicing, the power of the wonders, and the works of God, as we celebrate the power of the Lord.

Lord, we worship you, and we praise you. We proclaim that every day is special for us.

Lord, we thank you that all that we do is God's work. We rub our eyes, because we hardly believe it. It's so good.

---

1. ESV

We have an abundant life, a good life. God is at work in us and through us.

This is the very day God acted. So we are celebrating; we are festive.

We thank you for your presence in us. Thank you for a fresh anointing.

This is the day—every day is the day—that the Lord has made. We rejoice and are glad in it.

Thank you, Lord, for your power on us and your spirit resting in us. Thank you, Lord, for the Spirit of the Lord that's upon us.

As *The Aramaic Bible in Plain English* says: "This is the day that LORD JEHOVAH has made; come, we will leap for joy and rejoice in him!"

We celebrate his faithfulness. We celebrate the victory we have in Christ.

We are happy because we have been born again. And we're glad.

Father, we come into the courts of the Lord, and we praise you, we worship you, and we celebrate you.

Lord, we do thank you for your spirit being upon us. Lord, you have faithfully carried us. Lord, you are watching over us, directing us.

Your hand is upon us. You are opening up opportunities for us. Lord, you're giving us a grace to fulfill our call.

Lord, as we enter into a new season, a new year of life, Lord, we thank you that we are going to finish strong this year. We're going to be energized. We're going to be passionate. We're going to be full of power, full of favor, full of experience, full of knowledge and understanding. You give generously to all.

Lord, we come as your servant. You died on the cross for us so that we can live, and not just live, but live the abundant life.

Lord, we give you our all, because you gave your all for us.

Lord, we thank you for your Spirit being upon us. Thank you for creativity. Bless us this day with peace and joy, grace and favor. Amen.

5

DAY 5

PSALM 3:3-4

*B*ut you, LORD, are a shield around me, my glory, the One *who lifts my head high.*

I call out to the LORD, and he answers me from his holy mountain.

This Psalm of David recalls the time when David was fleeing from Jerusalem as his rebellious son Absalom was trying to claim his throne.[1]

Lord, we thank you for this psalm of David, that you are with us. You are a shield around us, Lord, the glory that rests on us, and the one who lifts up our head.

I cry aloud, and he answers me.

Lord, thank you for prayer. Thank you for the power that comes as we exalt your name and cry out to you. Thank you

---

1. See II Samuel chapters 15, 16, and 17.

that in the midst of enemies—whether the spiritual enemies of our soul, or flesh and blood enemies who make life difficult—you provide divine protection.

Lord, thank you for you being the Eternal One who wraps us with an impenetrable shield, a bulletproof shield, that nothing can shatter or penetrate.

You give your glory to us. You lift our head. You respond to us; you answer us quickly.

Father, thank you for the favor of God upon us, that as we cry out to you, you hear and respond quickly.

Lord, you are our shield, you are our glory, you are our hope.

You alone are our defender and protector. Strengthen us. Empower us.

You are the one that lifts up our head.

Father, thank you that you provide a shield for us on all sides. You ground our feet on the rock of Christ, and you lift our head high.

With all our might, we shout out to God: "My God is more than enough! My God provides! My God reveals! My God guides!"

He answers us with thunder from his holy mountain.

Father, we celebrate that you are with us. We celebrate your presence. We celebrate your power. We celebrate your glory.

Lord, you are our shield. You guard our heart. You guard our mind. You guard our body.

You are the one who defends us and protects us. Lord, we ask you to be with us. We don't have to hang our head in shame or guilt or fear or condemnation.

Lord, at no point today do we need to hang our head as if you aren't with us.

Thank you for always hearing our prayers and answering us.

I pray, Jesus, that you be glorified in us and through us, as we delight to walk with you.

Be with us in any storm and any battle.

You are the Lord our God who defends us and protects us. You are our shield.

Lord, we thank you. We love you and we praise you, and we celebrate the grace of God. Amen.

6

DAY 6

ISAIAH 43:2

*W*hen *you pass through the waters, I will be with you; and when you pass through the rivers, they will not sweep over you. When you walk through the fire, you will not be burned; the flames will not set you ablaze.*

Lord, thank you that we do not have to fear, for you have redeemed us. You have summoned us by name. You have called us, Lord.

Lord, you say that we are spiritually adopted. We are part of your chosen ones, part of your redemption, and even in time of trial or tribulation testing, even in a time of affliction, Lord, your presence is with us.

Your promise is with us. The supernatural care of God. Thank you that you're with us, Lord, in every season.

Lord, as it says in *The Voice*, "When you face *stormy* seas I will be there with you *with endurance and calm*; you will not be engulfed in *raging* rivers. If *it seems like* you're walking through fire with flames *licking at your limbs, keep going;* you won't be burned."

Lord, even when we walk through the fire, with flames licking at our limbs, we can keep going, for you are with us. God, we want to thank you for giving us more—another day, another year—to live for you.

Thank you that you are giving us this season, this productive season, this efficient and effective season, when you are bringing our lives in order, our families in order, to advance your kingdom and bring you glory.

God, thank you that this world doesn't define us, but you do. Thank you for being with us, even when we have felt overwhelmed, even when circumstances and situations and feelings and emotions threaten to overtake us.

Lord, you have helped us pass through many trials, many tribulations, and even many fires. And yet we are not burned. We don't smell like smoke.

Thank you, Father, that you shed your blood to give us the covenant of blessings of youthfulness and vitality, of energy and passion. Thank you for the fresh wind of God. We don't have to be afraid. You have redeemed us. We are yours.

Lord, when we feel over our heads, you will be with us.

When we are in difficult, turbulent situations, with rough waters, Lord, we are not going down.

When we are between a rock and a hard place, even when it looks like a dead end for us, you are with us, God. You are our

Savior. You paid a huge price for us. And you are working on our behalf.

Lord, even in seasons, where there's difficulties, where navigation is hard, you will be with us. When we goes through times of difficulties. Lord, we won't go down. We won't be pulled down. We will not drown. Lord, when we are going through the fire of oppression and difficulties and trials, we won't be burned up. The flames will not consume us.

Lord, thank you that you give us another year so we can glorify you. We love you, Father. We love you, Jesus. We love you, Holy Spirit.

We love your word, and we love bringing you honor and glory.

Be with us, Lord. Show us your divine care. Show us your presence and reveal your ways to us.

In Jesus' name. Amen.

7

DAY 7

COLOSSIANS 3:15

L *et the peace of Christ rule in your hearts, since as members of one body you were called to peace. And be thankful.*

I proclaim this as a blessing over your life, as the Amplified says: "Let the peace of Christ [the inner calm of one who walks daily with Him] be the controlling factor in your hearts [deciding and settling questions that arise]. To this *peace* indeed you were called as members in one body [of believers]. And be thankful [to God always]."

May the peace that comes from Christ rule in our hearts. As a member of one body, we are called to live in peace, the sensitivity to the Spirit that the Lord has given us.

The peace, the shalom of God, will help us navigate this day. God's peace will help us to decide and settle questions that arise. As believers in Christ, we have been called to this peace. We are always thankful for the peace of Messiah, that it would govern our hearts, will rule our hearts. It will lead us and guide us; it will refresh us and restore us.

It will work as a navigation system, give us a spiritual GPS. The peace of Christ will be part of our discernment, help guide us in the decisions we make.

We will be governed by the peace. Our discernment will be in alignment with the peace. We will be unsettled when we aren't in alignment. When the Lord says, "Don't go to the right," or, "go to the left," or "speed up," or "slow down"—God's peace will help guide our hearts.

I proclaim the peace of the anointing, the governing of the anointing. Your hearts will be guided by it.

Lord, I thank you that the peace of Christ keeps us in tune with the will of God. The peace of Christ keeps us in tune with each other, helps us to be in step with others.

I proclaim that you are going to have an upgrade of being in step with Jesus and knowing his guidance for your own life, and for family, friends, business associates, and clients.

A whole new upgrade of discernment is coming, through the governing of the peace of Christ.

Lord, I bless us with the upgrade. I bless us with insight. I pray for us for this breaker anointing of seeing and determining which way to go for our lives and for others, through the rule, the rod, and the peace. May we be ever guided by the peace of the Anointed One. Amen.

Bless you, child of God. Peace and grace be with you.

8

DAY 8

PHILIPPIANS 4:7

A *nd the peace of God, which transcends all understanding,*
will guard your hearts and your minds in Christ Jesus.

Father, I thank you for the supernatural experience of God's peace that we receive. Your peace will guard our hearts and minds in Christ Jesus. This supernatural download, this peace that reassures the heart, the shalom of God that transcends all understanding, stands guard over hearts and minds in Christ Jesus.

And it is ours.

Lord, I thank you for this gift, a sense of God's wholeness, a sense of everything coming together for good, a settling down, Lord, of being able to celebrate every day. We have God's provision, we are God's workmanship, and we are in God's hand.

Lord, I thank you, for the grace of God that allows us not to fret or worry, but to find calmness in the center of your will.

We get to be guided with peace instead of worries and fear. Thank you, Lord, for this.

Lord, your peace transcends our understanding. Thank you that you are guiding and directing.

Thank you that the peace of El Shaddai is upon us, the peace that is beyond any and all human understanding guards us.

May we enter into a fullness of abundance of the peace of God. Amen.

9

DAY 9

PSALM 144:1-2

*P*raise be to the Lord my Rock, who trains my hands for war,
my fingers for battle.

*He is my loving God and my fortress, my stronghold and my
deliverer, my shield, in whom I take refuge, who subdues peoples
under me.*

Lord, you are not only the one who protects us like a shield,
but you also give us weapons to fight with. You give us the two
edged sword to swing, Lord, to swing it and to use it.

And Lord, you gifted each of us with specific gifts for us.
Thank you, Lord, for this blessing that's upon us.

I speak favor, favor favor.

Lord, thank you that we're going to have greater power to
cut through those things that put others in bondage. And
Lord, you're going to give us an amazing creativity and inspi-
ration with spiritual weapons to encourage people in faith.

Thank you for your divine protection upon us. God, you prepared us for the battles that come our way.

Protect our minds. Lord, give us the upgrade of the mind of Christ. Guide us with insight and wisdom and revelation.

Lord, I pray Psalm 144 as a blessing. Lord, we want the same gift that Jesus had: give us the Spirit of the Lord, the Spirit of wisdom and of understanding, the Spirit of counsel and of might, the Spirit of the knowledge and fear of the Lord.

Lord, please bless us. You are the rock, and you train us. May your divine protection be upon us. Lord, bless us indeed. In Jesus' name. Amen.

God has trained us for such a time as this. May we go forth in the power of the Spirit.

10

DAY 10

PSALM 100

S *hout for joy to the LORD, all the earth.*
      Worship the LORD with gladness; come before him with joyful songs.

Know that the LORD is God. It is he who made us, and we are his; we are his people, the sheep of his pasture.

Enter his gates with thanksgiving and his courts with praise; give thanks to him and praise his name.

For the LORD is good and his love endures forever; his faithfulness continues through all generations.

One of the best known and most loved of all the Psalms, this hymn of thanksgiving.

We're invited by God to come into his temple and enter into the sacred place with joy and with gratitude.

We can be so thankful and have such joy because we're God's created sons and daughters. We're part of his gracious act of love. He's made us his own people. He's chosen us. He loves us. He calls us unique, wonderfully and fearfully made. We're God's sheep in his fold. We're living in his pasture.

What a great song, full of the triumph found in confidence and hope in God.

The Lord is faithful and true. He's eternal. He's good. His love and faithfulness remain forever.

Lord, thank you that you are the eternal one, the true God.

Lord, we're your people, like sheep, grazing in your fields. We've gone through your gates. We walk through your courts, giving thanks and praise.

We offer gratitude to you with all our hearts. We praise your name.

Lord, our life and identity and purpose is found in you.

The Eternal One, the great I am is good. His love is loyal. His mercy never ends. His truth lasts from one generation to the next.

Lord, we enter the gates of the Lord with thanksgiving. We go through these open gates. Your blood has purchased the work on the cross, and your resurrection provides the great thanksgiving.

We give thanks to you and bless your holy name.

We enter with the password, "Thank you."

In Jesus' name, amen.

11

DAY 11

III John 2

*D ear friend, I pray that you may enjoy good health and
that all may go well with you, even as your soul is getting
along well.*

In *The Voice*, this verse says, "My beloved friend, I pray that
everything is going well for you and that your body is as healthy
as your soul is prosperous."

I am thinking about the power of being his beloved, and the
value of being his beloved.

Don't feel bad when things don't seem to be working out as
you had hoped, or desired, or wished. Don't feel bad if things
are moving at a snail's pace, slow, or maybe even feel stalled.

Be encouraged this day, beloved of God: the snail is still
moving, drops in a bucket add up, and the bucket will even-
tually overflow.

Beloved, don't grow weary of doing what is right, for in due time, you'll reap a harvest of blessings.

Don't stop trying. Don't stop working at it. Keep moving forward.

No matter what keeps backing up, no matter what delays, don't slow down, and don't stay down.

Each of us have wins and losses. But if you ever interview a research doctor, a scientist, a creative person, or even an entrepreneur, they will tell you that many times they failed, how many attempts have failed, how many tries they missed before they got it right.

I think of the saying, "Swing for the fences!"

In Major League Baseball, when a player swings for the fences, this increases his strikeout ratio.

But the player also gets bigger and better hits, which means more runs. More runs allows a team to win more.

Lord, thank you for your beloved. Lord, may we enjoy the journey with you, even if we tend to be destination people. May we not begrudge the process.

Jesus, you said, "With God, all things are possible."[1]

So, Lord, may we not give up too early. May we keep moving forward, as your beloved. Amen.

---

1. Matthew 19:26

12

DAY 12

Psalm 67:1

*M*ay God be gracious to us and bless us and make his face shine on us.

This verse echoes Numbers 6:24-26, the blessing God gave to Aaron and his sons, with which to bless the people.

I once had a dream in which I heard a voice, and several voices, speak and sing Psalm 67:1 over me, and I speak this blessing over you, like the Lord spoke it to me and over me.

God, keep us near your mercy fountain and bless us.

And when you look down on us, may your face beam with joy, and Lord pause in his presence of his blessing. Lord, I thank you that you are blessing us with your gracious presence.

Lord, you have a whole new realm for us of the discoveries of your love for us. We are your beloved.

May you favor us, and extend your mercy and grace to us, and add a greater knowledge of you, Lord. Release your face, your image, the brightness of your glory. May your face appear as a blessing to us. May it shine forth, as the face of God reflects off of us.

Father, we thank you for the mercy of God.

Lord, I speak this blessing, Psalm 67:1.

"May God have pity on us and bless us! May he smile on us. *Selah.*"[1]

"May God be gracious to us and bless us; look on us with favor. *Selah.*"[2]

Lord, we thank you, Father, that you are being gracious to us and blessing us. You're causing your face to shine upon us. Lord, be merciful. Be gracious, be kind, be generous upon us.

Make our faces shine with favor on it.

Lord, you blessed me, and I bless others. May the favor of God rest upon us. May your unconditional love invite us to deep friendship as your beloved.

God, bless us with your peace. Bless us with your joy.

In the fullness of the Father, Son and the Holy Spirit's blessing. In Jesus name. Amen.

---

1. God's Word Translation

2. Holman Christian Standard Bible

13

DAY 13

I Samuel 3:10

T he LORD came and stood there, calling as at the other times, "Samuel! Samuel!"
Then Samuel said, "Speak, for your servant is listening."

The Lord was needing a prophet, a seer for that age, for that season.

The Lord speaks to each of us. We have the possibility to recognize divine encounters.

Lord, visit us with desire, with hunger and longing to know your voice, to be a seer, to be a speaker for him.

Lord, may we have a willing heart, a listening ear, to comprehend what you're saying.

Speak, for thy servant heareth.

Speak, for your servant is listening.

Speak, for your bondservant is here, willing to do what you say and speak.

I'm listening, Lord. What do you want from me? What are you asking me?

Lord, you have a great call for each one of us. Lord, we're listening. We have a willing heart, open hands, and a listening ear. And so the word of the Lord is going to be revealed in a greater amount.

Lord, you're going to reveal the next phase of your activity. You're going to reveal prophetic power. You're going to confirm our words with signs and wonders. Prophetic credibility is being established at a new level in our lives. Thank you, Lord, for this blessing.

The Lord comes to each of us and says, "My beloved, the one who brings joy and hope and faith to others."

And we can respond, "Yes, Lord. I'm listening. I'm willing. Speak. I'm your servant. I'm ready to listen. Speak, Lord, I'm your friend. I'm here. Speak, oh, eternal one. Your child is listening."

Lord, bless these willing hearts.

Lord, bless these minds to be able to comprehend.

Bless these ears to hear what the Holy Spirit is saying.

Lord, bless us with the gift of discerning the seasons and the times.

Lord, bless us indeed.

May our ears hear. May our hearts be strengthened. And may you develop the prophetic call on your servant. Strengthen the seer gift, the hearing ear, and the listening heart. In Jesus' name. Amen.

14

DAY 14

SONG OF SONGS 8:6-7

Place me like a seal over your heart, like a seal on your arm; for love is as strong as death, its jealousy unyielding as the grave. It burns like blazing fire, like a mighty flame.

Many waters cannot quench love; rivers cannot sweep it away. If one were to give all the wealth of one's house for love, it would be utterly scorned.

Thank you for the greater measure of revelation that we are your beloved. As *The Message* says: "Hang my locket around your neck, wear my ring on your finger. Love is invincible facing danger and death. Passion laughs at the terrors of hell. The fire of love stops at nothing—it sweeps everything before it. Flood waters can't drown love, torrents of rain can't put it out. Love can't be bought, love can't be sold - it's not to be found in the marketplace."

Thank you that the fire of your love stops at nothing. Thank you that your Spirit rests on us.

Thank you for your seal over our hearts. Thank you for the love of God that sets us apart and calls us chosen.

You put a seal on our hearts, a seal on our arms. Your love is as strong as death. Lord! So powerful! Your Spirit is so strong!

Thank you, Lord, that mighty waters cannot quench this love.

The Passion Translation reads like this.

> Fasten me upon your heart as a seal of fire forevermore. This living, consuming flame will seal you as my prisoner of love. My passion is stronger than the chains of death and the grave, all consuming as the very flashes of fire from the burning heart of God.
>
> Place this fierce, unrelenting fire over your entire being.
>
> Rivers of pain and persecution will never extinguish this flame. Endless floods will be unable to quench this raging fire that burns within you. Everything will be consumed. It will stop at nothing as you yield everything to this furious fire until it won't even seem to you like a sacrifice anymore.

Father, bless us with the seal of God's love, like a seal on our arms. Oh God, do a great work with this seal.

May your love be as strong as anything we have ever experienced, the flaming fire of God. Lord, let the blazing fire and the flame of the Lord be upon us.

May many waters not quench this love. Lord, may nothing stop the love of God that is ever growing, the love of the Father, the love of the Son, and the Holy Spirit.

Lord, do a great work in us.

We are your beloved. Fasten upon our hearts, the seal of the fiery love of God. The love of Papa, the love of Jesus, and the love of Holy Spirit. Lord, seal us with this love. May your passionate arms be around us. May we sense your strong sense of being blessed as your beloved. Lord, place your fierce, unrelenting fire over our entire being. Lord, let the flood of your love be upon us.

Bless us with your presence, more of your love, more of your wrap-around presence.

Lord, may this be the year of breakthrough. May this be the year of kingdom acceleration. May this be the year of the hand of favor being up us, the breakthrough year, as your beloved, secure in your arms.

Lord, release your favor to new levels before us. Let us walk securely. Let us work confidently. And, Lord, let us enter into a whole new area of confidence, clarity, and courage.

Release more of your fire, more of your fire, more of your fire. Let that heart be on fire. Bless us with fresh passion for Jesus. Amen and Amen.

15

DAY 15

PHILIPPIANS 4:7

A *nd the peace of God, which transcends all understanding, will guard your hearts and your minds in Christ Jesus.*

One of my favorite verses, one that I love to pray over myself, I'm speaking over you, from *The Message*: "Before you know it, a sense of God's wholeness, everything coming together for good, will come and settle you down. It's wonderful what happens when Christ displaces worry at the center of your life."

Wow.

Father, we thank you for your word. Thank you for your presence. Thank you for the wonderful peace that transcends human understanding, and guards our hearts and minds through Christ Jesus.

Lord, may we be saturated in prayer, covered by the love of God. May the wraparound presence saturate us, filling us, empowering us.

Thank you, Holy Spirit, for your presence being in us and through us, and the peace of God, which transcends all understanding, guards our hearts and minds in Christ Jesus.

And as this blessing comes to fulfillment, we experience new levels of peace that exceed anything and everything we've ever experienced before. Our hearts and minds are being encountered with the *shalom* of God as we live and walk in Christ Jesus.

Yes. The peace of God, the *shalom* of God, the goodness of God, the grace of God rest upon us.

I bless you with the love of God. I bless you with this peace, which reassures your heart, the *shalom*, that transcends all understanding. Yes, it's from Yeshua, the Messiah, because you belong to Christ Jesus. God will bless you with peace.

You are entering into a new realm of confidence, security, and the wraparound presence of God.

The *shalom* of God. It guards your hearts and minds in Christ Jesus. Amen.

16

DAY 16
ROMANS 8:31, 37

What, then, shall we say in response to these things? If God is for us, who can be against us? No, in all these things we are more than conquerors through him who loved us.

I speak God's love over you. If God is for you, who can be against you? You are more than a conqueror in Christ Jesus.

More than a conqueror? That means you are inevitable, that you are impossible to stop. You're a born winner, set apart by God to be number one. Not number two, not number three, not number four.

Not just close, like in horseshoes.

But you are called and destined to be a winner, a champion. The odds are for you.

Bursting with confidence, walking in the favor and the strength of God, seen and obvious to all.

You are going to have a whole new work of grace in you, and upgrade of the work of the mercy, the grace, and the favor of God.

You are his beloved, and there is a divine call on your life.

You are part of the royal priesthood.

You are chosen by God and for God.

You are foreordained, predestined, wonderfully and fearfully made, a masterpiece.

And in all things, you are more than a conqueror, through Christ who loves you. Spiritual victory is for you.

Assurance of love is found in Christ. Assurance of victory is discovered in Christ. Assurance of God's protection is part of your upgrade.

If God is for you, who can be against you?

Yes, you are royally blessed and highly favored of the Lord. I proclaim this blessing over you.

Amen.

17

DAY 17

ROMANS 8:15-17

The Spirit you received does not make you slaves, so that you live in fear again; rather, the Spirit you received brought about your adoption to sonship. And by him we cry, "Abba, Father." The Spirit himself testifies with our spirit that we are God's children. Now if we are children, then we are heirs—heirs of God and co-heirs with Christ, if indeed we share in his sufferings in order that we may also share in his glory.

Some of my favorite passages of scripture, that I prayed over myself for years, I extend now over you.

The royal blood is flowing through you. You are a child of the Most High God. That's been my prayer, my paraphrased version of Romans 8:15-17: "The royal blood of Christ flows through me as a child of the Most High God."

Or, in the *New Living Translation*: "So you have not received a spirit that makes you fearful slaves. Instead, you received God's Spirit when he adopted you as his own children. Now we call him, 'Abba, Father.' For his Spirit joins with our spirit to affirm that we are God's children."

You not received the spirit of fear. Instead, you receive God's Spirit, which adopted you as his own child. He called you. Now you can call him, "Papa, Daddy."

Thank you, Lord.

Lord, this resurrection life lives in us. It's not timid. It's not shallow. It's not grave-tending.

No. It's the life of God. It's the adventure of being a child of God.

Lord, stir up the adventurous spirit. "What's next, Papa God? What's next for your child?"

May God's Spirit touch your spirit and confirm over and over, that you are blessed as his child.

You know who you are, and know where you're going.

You have a great inheritance.

So even if you go through the hard times, you can trust the Lord, that he is with you.

You are an heir of God, and a co-heir with Christ. You are royalty. You are royally blessed. The royal blood flows through you. You're a child of the Most High God. You are highly favored. And you are celebrated.

18

DAY 18

NUMBERS 6:24-26

The LORD bless you and keep you;
*   the LORD make his face shine on you and be gracious*
to you;
*   the LORD turn his face toward you and give you peace.*

What a blessing!

Taking phrases from a number of translations: The LORD bless you and watch over you, guard you and keep you. The LORD make his face to shine upon you and enlighten you and be gracious to you. The LORD be kind to you, merciful to you, and giving to you much, much favor. The LORD lift up his approving countenance upon you, and give you great peace, tranquillity of heart, and life continually.[1]

---

1. biblehub.com offers each verse in a number of different translations ... a great resource!

I proclaim as God's child, you are encouraged as you experience God's sovereignty over your life, beyond what your eyes can see, or even heart can even imagine.

. God has blessings in store for you.

Yes, the stresses of life challenge us: work, family, health, relationships. Sometimes we're challenged. Sometimes we're overwhelmed.

However, in all this, God intentionally is watching over you. He's all powerful. And he's able to do exceedingly, abundantly more than all that you ask, or even think or imagine.

The doors God chooses to open in your life leave you standing in awe at times. He can also close the doors that he feels aren't the right time for you.

So be encouraged, child, that the greatest blessings are coming for you. And don't be discouraged in a time of testing or trial. For then we experience that God will turn things around. He makes every crooked path straight. He turns our mourning into dancing. He turns our trials into triumphs.

You are a child of the most high God, one of his people, the sheep of his pasture.

The power of this prayer of blessing is going to transform your life, your family, your work, your ministry, your business, as well as your gifts, calling, and abilities.

For you are called to be blessed and highly favored. God watches over his word to perform it. And he's watching over you. He's made you an instrument for him. You have the Spirit of the Lord on you. As one that walks in revelation and insight, you're going to anoint others.

There's going to be an atomic blessing being released from you.

You have a great future.

The Lord bless you and keep you. The *shalom* of God be upon you. In Jesus' name, amen.

19

DAY 19

DEUTERONOMY 7:9

*K*now therefore that the LORD your God is God; he is the
*faithful God, keeping his covenant of love to a thousand
generations of those who love him and keep his commandments.*

Lord, we thank you for yesterday's blessing, the Numbers
6 blessing, and I prolong that blessing, partnering it with
Deuteronomy 7:9.

"May the LORD bless you and take care of you; May the
LORD be kind and gracious to you; May the LORD look on
you with favor and give you peace."[1]

Then combine that with Deuteronomy 7:9, where God
shows his love to a thousand generations of those who love
him.

That's you. And that's your family.

---

1. Numbers 6:24-26 (GNT)

Take this blessing: because you love him, may his favor be upon you to a thousand generations: for your family and your children and their children and their children's children.

The Voice translation says, "I want you to know that the Eternal your God is *the only true* God. He's the faithful God who keeps His covenants and shows loyal love for a thousand generations to those who *in return* love Him and keep His commands."

As you follow God's words, the Lord pours out his intense love, his blessing: out of sheer love, keeping his promises from one generation to the next.

Lord, I proclaim, in Jesus' name, your blessing for a thousand generations.

Lord, we proclaim that your purposes are being released.

May the Lord bless you, guide you, and protect you. May that which the Lord desires find expression in you. May your life generate peace; may your words release life, and healing, and hope.

As part of the body of Christ, may you be a light that shines.

And may the blessing of the Lord be upon you as never before.

The Lord bless you in your day-to-day. Amen.

20

DAY 20

LUKE 1:37

For no word from God will ever fail.

The Lord sent his angel to proclaim over Mary, "Nothing is impossible for God!"[1]

As the angel spoke to Mary, I proclaim that God does not change, and so nothing is impossible with God for us, his people.

Holy Spirit, rest upon us. May your divine ability be manifest in our lives. May your omnipotence multiply, in our lives, your presence, and your power, and your spirit.

May we have an increase of faith for the supernatural, miracles, and the miraculous.

God, you can do all things.

May we experience an increase of power of the Spirit.

---

1. Contemporary English Version

Lord, may you do more than what we could ask, think, or imagine.

The things which are impossible with men and women are possible with God, because nothing is too difficult for God. Nothing is impossible for God. Nothing is impossible with respect to any of God's promises.

With God, nothing is, and nothing ever shall be, impossible.

Lord, we speak the blessing of God, the supernatural ability, the angelic provision, the supernatural help of God.

For Lord, with you, nothing will be impossible. Do more in our lives than we ever thought or dreamed or conceived.

For with God, nothing shall be impossible.

Bless us with favor. Bless us with the peace and the glory of the Lord. May it rest upon us. In Jesus' name, amen.

21

DAY 21
PSALM 63:1

You, God, are my God, earnestly I seek you; I thirst for you, my whole being longs for you, in a dry and parched land where there is no water.

One of my life passages. Praying for your hunger and your thirst, and humility. Hunger and humility: the currency of heaven.

On December 3, 2004, a Friday, I heard Bill Johnson preach for the first time. He spoke at Grace Center in Franklin, Tennessee, and it changed my life. He preached from Psalm 63:1, and he talked about the water level, the water table, and how important it is to thirst.

When he looked at Franklin in 2004, the water level was low. "There's not enough hunger and thirst," he said.

He came every year around this time, the weekend after Thanksgiving.

Ten years later, in 2014, he said, "Now the water level has has risen. There's greater hunger for God, greater thirst for the Lord."

Lord, I proclaim this blessing over each one: you are chosen by Jehovah. You are a seeker after God. You're a God-Chaser. You thirst, like a deer panting for water.

Jesus said, "Blessed are those who hunger and thirst for righteousness, for they will be filled."[1]

Yes, this is your spiritual desire: for more of him. You've cried out God, "You are my God! I can't get enough of you! I've worked up such a hunger and thirst for God, but Lord, I'm thirsty for more!"

Father, as your children have earnestly searched for you, Lord, longed for you, as they are thirsty, Lord, would you give them the water that they need.

The Passion Translation says, "O God of my life, I'm lovesick for you in this weary wilderness. I thirst with the deepest longings to love you more, with cravings in my heart that can't be described. Such yearning grips my soul for you, my God!"

Lord, grant this prayer. Bless your children with more of your presence, more of your Spirit, more of the anointing of intimacy with the Lord, more of the breakthrough.

Lord, we're asking that you do this in a greater measure for your children, as they cry out, "Abba, Papa," would you meet

---

1. Matthew 5:6

each one, encounter, and fill, with your glory, your Spirit and your blessing?

As his beloved, he is placing hunger and thirst in you to new measures. In Jesus' name. Amen.

22

DAY 22

II CORINTHIANS 13:14

*M*ay the grace of the Lord Jesus Christ, and the love of God, and the fellowship of the Holy Spirit be with you all.

The last verse of Paul's second letter to the Corinthians, a book that could be called "The New Life in God."

I've been praying this verse for 40 years, ever since a prayer meeting in Gainesville, Florida, at a gathering of pastors as we were praying, singing, and worshiping.

In the New American Standard Bible, which was the translation I was using then: "The grace of the Lord Jesus Christ, and the love of God, and the fellowship of the Holy Spirit, be with you all."

I speak this blessing: now may the grace and joyous favor of the Lord Jesus Christ be with you.

May this unexplainable, powerful, clear, obvious, unblurred explicit love of God the Father be with you.

May the precious communion that we all share in the Holy Spirit, be yours continually.

I proclaim this over you as one of God's chasers: your spiritual thirst for him, the hunger and thirst and desire, is beautiful.

So I pray for greater friendship and fellowship with the Holy Spirit, greater communion with God, an amazing friendship with the Holy Spirit, one of deep friendship, one of a life-changing, beautiful friendship, true communion with the Holy Spirit, intimate friendship of the Holy Spirit.

I speak over you this amazing grace of our master and King, the Lord Jesus, in the amazing, extravagant love of Papa God.

Grace and favor multiplies by walking with your master, your friend, the King, Jesus, Savior, and Christ, the Anointed One, who breaks the yokes and sets the captives free.

I proclaim this grace and this blessing, this benediction over you. Amen.

23

DAY 23

PHILIPPIANS 3:13-14

*B*rothers and sisters, I do not consider myself yet to have taken hold of it. But one thing I do: Forgetting what is behind and straining toward what is ahead, I press on toward the goal to win the prize for which God has called me heavenward in Christ Jesus.

I preached this as my very first sermon at a church service, Sunday evening, in September 1981, and I would have used this translation: "Brethren, I do not regard myself as having laid hold of it yet; but one thing I do: forgetting what lies behind and reaching forward to what lies ahead, I press on toward the goal for the prize of the upward call of God in Christ Jesus."[1]

Lord, I thank you for your precious Word.

---

1. NASB

Lord, I bless your people with the heart of a champion.

Lord, we're pursuing you. Teach us to measure our spiritual progress as we continue to walk forward, with great spiritual ambition, striving to win in this race, this calling on our lives.

Thank you for the strong, spiritual and godly ambitions you've given us. Thank you, Father, that the Holy Spirit has set us apart, sanctified us.

Thank you for minds and hearts that desire to walk in the fullness of the call of God on our lives. We thank you, Father, for the grace of the Lord Jesus.

Lord, we haven't taken possession of it yet, but we're pursuing it. We don't depend on our own strength to accomplish this. Our hearts are completely focused on you.

But as we forget the past, as we fasten our heart to the future ahead, trusting you, believing you, walking with you, Lord, bless us indeed.

As we accept the invitation to run the race with the heavenly goal in gaining the victory prize, through the anointing of Jesus, you pronounce us winners. We are going to get the prize. As we have lived life focused on the goal, Lord, we will obtain what you want us to.

Thank you, Father.

Lord, as we press in, we see God beckoning us onward to Jesus.

We are often running. Not turning back.

Lord, as we are focused on the goal, bless us, Lord. May we be your champions for Christ. Bless us, Lord, and keep us.

Make your face shine as we search for you, as we press into you. May you be gracious to us, as we give our all to seek your face, to use our gifts and talents for you.

To God be the glory. Amen.

24

DAY 24

EPHESIANS 3:20

Now to him who is able to do immeasurably more than all we ask or imagine, according to his power that is at work within us.

Lord, thank you for spiritual fullness. Thank you for fullness in Christ. Thank you for the supernatural power that releases divine ability. Thank you for supernatural abundance coming in our lives. Thank you for the providence of God, the hand of God that's on our lives.

Heavenly Father, we thank you that you are able to do exceedingly, abundantly above all that we ask or think or even imagine.

Thank you, Holy Spirit, that you are releasing supernatural power upon us. Work this miracle in us. Lord, yield a great fruit in our lives. Release a harvest, Lord, that's beyond our imagination. Do more than what we could think or imagine,

Lord. Do infinitely more. Beyond our greatest prayers, our greatest hopes, our greatest dreams.

Lord, you are working actively and powerfully in us.

Now, Father, we trust you for the supernatural. We trust you for the power. We trust you for the greatness.

Lord, we thank you for this amazing blessing, the power that is beyond understanding, the favor that's being released in our lives.

Lord, we know that you can do far more than what we could ever imagine, guess, or even request, in our wildest dreams.

Lord, we're asking that you bless us indeed, that you prosper us, that your favor will be upon us, the anointing will be upon us, the presence, the power, Lord, your supernatural help.

We pray all this in Jesus' name. Amen, amen, and amen.

25

DAY 25

Psalm 121

A song of ascents. I lift up my eyes to the mountains—where does my help come from?

My help comes from the LORD, the Maker of heaven and earth.

He will not let your foot slip—he who watches over you will not slumber;

indeed, he who watches over Israel will neither slumber nor sleep.

The LORD watches over you—the LORD is your shade at your right hand;

the sun will not harm you by day, nor the moon by night.

The LORD will keep you from all harm—he will watch over your life;

the LORD will watch over your coming and going both now and forevermore.

One of my favorite Psalms, a song for those journeying to worship. Eight short verses.

In *The Voice* translation:

"I look up at the *vast size of the* mountains—from where will my help come *in times of trouble*?

The Eternal Creator of heaven and earth *and these mountains* will send the help I need.

He holds you firmly in place; He will not let you fall. He who keeps you will *never take His eyes off you and* never drift off to sleep.

What a relief! The One who watches over Israel never leaves for rest or sleep.

The Eternal keeps you safe, *so close to Him that His shadow* is a *cooling* shade to you.

Neither bright light of sun nor dim light of moon will harm you.

The Eternal will keep you safe from all of life's evils,

From your first breath to the last breath you breathe, from this day and forever."

Lord, we thank you for the supernatural protection of God. We thank you for your protection. We thank you for your provision.

Lord, as we look to you, the divine helper shows up. The Creator guides and directs us.

Lord, I declare this blessing of your providence in our lives.

I proclaim the security of the Lord's protection and angelic help.

I speak safety. There's a protective providence of God for us. There's a protective shield around us. There's a divine care upon us. And there's a supernatural consistency in us.

You are the God who rescues. You are the God who provides.

Lord, our strength comes from you. You won't let us stumble. You won't let us fall. You are the one who protects us. You are the one who shields us.

You, Lord, who guides us and guards us, you will never leave us. You protect us and defend us. And so Lord, we're trusting you that as we cry out to you, you're bringing divine help.

Lord, our help comes from the Lord. Protection comes from the Lord. Guidance comes from the Lord. Provision comes from the Lord.

Our eyes are on you. And we declare, Lord, your help, your guidance. Like Jehoshaphat said: "We might be powerless, but our eyes are on you."[1]

We know that our help comes from you. As it says in Psalms 11:1: "In the LORD I take refuge."

Not abandoned.

Lord, you speak to your people: favor. Peace. Blessing.

May the peace of God guard our hearts and minds in Christ Jesus. May you bless us and provide for us as we are on this journey. Amen.

---

1. II Chronicles 20:12

26

DAY 26

GALATIANS 4:6

*B*ecause you are his sons, God sent the Spirit of his Son into our hearts, the Spirit who calls out, "Abba, Father."

From slavery to sonship.

Where we have been in bondage to the performance of religion, and of life, God does a supernatural work through his redemption, through spiritual adoption, by the use of his Holy Spirit, the Spirit indwelling.

God the Father speaks this blessing over the children of God, and the spiritual heirs, which includes you.

Thank you, Lord, for this word. Thank you for your presence. Thank you for the hope that we have in Christ. Thank you for your blessing.

Abba, Father, thank you for loving us. Thank you for adopting us. Thank you for paying such a high cost for us to be in your family, the family of God.

You continue to remind us of our value.

Thank you, Father, for giving us the Spirit to cry out and say, "Abba, Father!" God sent the Spirit of his Son into our hearts. We have a relationship with him. We can call him, "Abba, Father," as sons and daughters, adopted by him. We have a legacy, a relationship with him, and a blessing.

Thank you, Father, for this blessing. We are part of God's royal family. We are highly favored. Set apart.

He speaks to us, and he communicates to us, and he reveals his promises: no longer slaves, to perform according to this world. We are free.

And because of the life of Christ, we can cry out intimately to him and say, "My Papa! My Papa!"

Thank you, Father, for this love. Thank you for doing such a great thing in us. Thank you for this work. Thank you for this blessing. Thank you for this gift. Amen.

27

DAY 27
PSALM 46:10

He says, "Be still, and know that I am God; I will be exalted among the nations, I will be exalted in the earth."

Glory to God!

The Passion Translation titles Psalm 46, "God on Our Side." God, the refuge of his people, the conqueror of his nations.

Verse 10: "Surrender your anxiety. Be still and realize that I am God. I am God above all the nations, and I am exalted throughout the whole earth."

This was one of the favorite Psalms of the great Martin Luther. He revolutionized the world with his realization that, through the Spirit of truth, the just shall live by faith. He had courage, and the spirit of might on him to set a spiritual revolution, as he thought through his 95 Theses, his thoughts, policies, principles.

Thank you, Father, for the spirit of might and power that you give to us as we sit and trust you. As we look to you, you are exalted.

Lord, bless us with peace, the shalom of God, as we return to you, day after day, and know that you are God. You will be exalted.

Thank you, Father, for the grace of God.

Thank you that the Lord of hosts is with us. Thank you that the Mighty God is with us.

Bless us with victory. Bless us with the power to impact the nations.

Lord, you are our refuge and strength. May the blessing of favor, may the Spirit of might and power, flow through us. Amen.

28

DAY 28

PSALM 90:17

May the favor of the Lord our God rest on us; establish the work of our hands for us—yes, establish the work of our hands.

Psalm 90, the only Psalm of Moses. He had seen 40 years in comfort in Egypt, then 40 years tending sheep in the desert, and then 40 years leading the people, wandering in the desert, as a whole generation squandered the promise.

He had a deep conviction that we must have a keen sense of time, as it swiftly passes. We must work for something significant. Make use of time.

Psalm 90:17 in *The Passion Translation* says, "O Lord our God, let your sweet beauty rest upon us. Come work with us, and then our works will endure; you will give us success in all we do."

Other translations use the word "favor" instead of "beauty."

Lord God, let your favor, your sweet favor, rest upon us.

Godspeed. God's work. God's glory. God's power.

That's your desire. And that's your blessing. You can rest assured, you can walk in the security of the blessing that your deeds are being shown to you as his servant. The splendor of the Lord will be displayed to you. The favor of the Lord will rest upon you. The spiritual blessings, the beauty, and speed no longer delay. No longer squandering time, but he is establishing the work of your life, your hands. Your time has come: like Moses, your time has come.

Lord, as we learn true wisdom, as we ask you for divine instruction, as we desire to be taught by the Holy Spirit, we ask for comfort and joy, as we walk in the beauty of the Lord God's favor.

Lord, we seek your face, and ask for the blessing of the mercy of God, the favor of God, the beauty of the Lord, to rest upon your servant.

We seek your face, Lord. Oh, Lord, your face is what we seek.

Lord, we praise the Eternal, that you are able to do it. We praise the Eternal One.

Lord, as we praise you, we join with angels above, we join with your people below, and all creations and all creatures in praising you.

I speak this blessing of favor, and the beauty of the Lord, with signs, and wonders, and miracles.

Lord, let the miracles once again flow. Let another generation see the glorious wonders of our King.

Father, you are Lord. May the beauty of the Lord, may the favor the Lord, may the gracious favor of God, rest upon us, and confirm the works of our hands. Yes, confirm the works.

Lord, we pray that your blessing will be upon us. Lord, bless us. Bless us. Bless us with favor, with the power of the resurrection, and with your wisdom. In Jesus' name. Amen.

29

DAY 29

PHILIPPIANS 4:8

Finally, brothers and sisters, whatever is true, whatever is noble, whatever is right, whatever is pure, whatever is lovely, whatever is admirable—if anything is excellent or praiseworthy—think about such things.

Lovely, lovely ... loving the blessings.

Lord, we're asking for your presence and your power, that this be the best year yet.

Lord, we seek your face for the blessing. Thank you, Father, for the blessings coming from this prayer and Philippians 4:8.

Lord, I proclaim, in Jesus' name, that we're so grateful for the oneness and unity reflected in the heart of the Father, Son, and Holy Spirit. Thank you for the power of agreement. Thank you for the supernatural symphony that our voices make together.

Lord, the release of heaven's power, kingdoms results, and the supernatural phenomenal impact of his presence and his power, his provision, and his purpose, and his peace that takes place as we partner together.

Lord, we do declare this blessing: "And now, dear brothers and sisters, one final thing. Fix your thoughts on what is accurate, and honorable, and right, and pure, and lovely, and admirable. Think about things that are excellent and worthy of praise."[1]

Lord, what a great blessing.

I remind you, children of God, "whatever is true, whatever is honorable *and* worthy of respect, whatever is right *and* confirmed by God's word, whatever is pure *and* wholesome, whatever is lovely *and* brings peace, whatever is admirable *and* of good repute; if there is any excellence, if there is anything worthy of praise, think *continually* on these things [center your mind on them, and implant them in your heart]."[2]

Thank you, Father, for the grace of God on us, that we can enter in to the blessing of Philippians 4:8.

Lord, bless us in our coming. Bless us in our going. Thank you for the power of agreement, the sound of the Lord that is made through our agreed prayer. Amen.

---

1. New Living Translation

2. Amplified

30

DAY 30
PSALM 37:4

Take delight in the Lord, and he will give you the desires of your heart.

The Lord means everything to you. You find peace, you find fulfillment in him.

He loves that about you.

He finds joy in your face, and in your pleasure in pursuit of him.

You live your life with the satisfaction of putting him first, of delighting in him. Your worth is found in Christ.

The Lord gives you the longing in your heart, draws you close to him. He blesses you, for your desire to rejoice in him, to delight yourself in the eternal things of God.

He sees your heart for rejoicing in his promises, even in the midst of a storm of disappointment, or resistance, or heartache, or frustration.

The Lord sees that you delight yourself in the eternal things of his heart, and his word, and his Spirit. You put him first. You've given him first place.

He finds pleasure in that.

He smiles on your face.

As you put him first, he finds pleasure in this. He finds joy. You've aligned your thoughts to his thoughts. You pray, "Not my will, but thy will, oh, God," and the desires of your heart continue to yield to his heart.

Even at times when you struggle to know his will, you're aligning your heart and your emotions with the eternal purposes and the perfect will of God.

Your delight in the Lord. You're given him first place. And the Lord says, "I'm going to bless you for that. I'm going to multiply the grace and mercy in your life. You're going to experience and encounter more of my steadfast love and faithfulness for putting me first."

The Lord says, "You're keeping company with the people of God. You're aligning your heart in the right way. I'm going to blessed that alignment. I'm going to bless you."

You have put delight in the ways of the Lord, and in worship. You've honored Yahweh. And he will give you what you desire the most. He's blessing you in your coming and going. You've taken great joy in his eternal heart, as the Alpha and Omega, the first and the last. You've lifted your hands to him in praise, and in cries. As you sing, ministering to the Lord, you sing a song of wisdom.

And he says, "I'm taking care of you. You're my child. The gifts are coming."

And he's lining them up with your heart's desire.

What a daily blessing as you open up your heart before God. You have honored him. You're keeping nothing back. And he'll do whatever needs to be done, for you are his child.

He's taking care of you. You put the hope of your heart in Lord Jehovah, and he's honoring the request of your heart. So I bless you with favor.

He will give you your heart's desire, and he's honoring your petitions.

So as you take delight in him, as you honor him, the King will bless you. As you abide in him, and his words abide in you, ask whatever you wish and it will be given to you.

The Lord takes delight in your praise. He takes delight in your heart. He blesses you with peace. He blesses you with prosperity. He blesses you with provision.

Do not envy those who do wrong, for the Lord will bless you. Do not envy those who are ahead of you or have more favor. For the Lord says, "You put your heart in my heart. You've delighted in me, and I will take care of you and give you the desires of your heart." Amen and amen.

31

DAY 31

MATTHEW 6:33-34

*B*ut seek first his kingdom and his righteousness, and all these things will be given to you as well. Therefore do not worry about tomorrow, for tomorrow will worry about itself. Each day has enough trouble of its own.

I bless you for putting God first: first in your life, first in your priorities. You're fulfilling the first commandment. Jesus spoke this, but the first of the Ten Commandments tells us to have no other gods before God. As you put God's kingdom first, you are not only walking by the Spirit, but you are walking in the instructions of Jesus.

You're putting your stake in the ground as you put God first, and say, "I'm not going to get distracted. I'm not going to get wayward. I'm walking in the truth."

In Christ, you can enjoy the abundant life.

You're establishing the habit of loving God's word, loving to talk to him and listen to him. Put him first: time in the Bible, seeking the Lord. Some times in our lives we have only a few minutes. At other times, we get more. But either way, you put God first.

It deepens your friendship with God.

You say, "I want to please you, Lord. I want to honor you. I want you to be first. I need you to help me to prioritize. I can't do it without the Lord. I can't do it on my own strength. I can't do it on my own ability."

The Lord says, "Yes. I promised to bless your life and make you prosper."

And the Lord is so gracious and kind. He knows when we miss the mark. He understands when we make mistakes.

Don't get discouraged. Don't let it hold you back. Keep going. God has given you the grace for what you will need to do today, and what you need to do in this season of your life, one day at a time.

Father, thank you for this blessing. Lord, we are prioritizing our lives to trust God. We're not going to sweat the small stuff. Because your kingdom, oh Lord, is paramount. We're seeking you first. Lord, we're asking Jesus to direct our steps, and trusting the Holy Spirit to guide us.

Thank you for your presence. Thank you for the grace of God.

As we put you first, this is the life of God worship.

Lord, you put us in this world. We pray for your protection, the protection of God's providence. Lord, as we seek God first, as we put you first, Lord, we trust you that you are blessing us.

We're asking for more of your blessing. We're asking for more of your peace and your protection. We're asking for the more of God as we put you first.

Jesus, loving Father, sometimes we are anxious, or we fret. We even, at times, have a lack of faith in your promise to take care of us and to provide.

But we put you first. We seek you first, and not the things of this world.

Father, forgive us for our lack of faith and trust in you.

I speak this blessing over your beloved, as we seek your kingdom and your righteousness first. Lord, we trust you, that you will be the great provider. As we seek the kingdom of God and his righteousness first, all these things will be given to us.

We don't have to worry about tomorrow. You even remind us that tomorrow has enough worries and anxiety.

Lord, we're going to live faithfully to you and put you first. We trust you.

As we do, you will work in our lives.

Father, we constantly seek you and your kingdom. Lord, we trust you.

Father, may the peace of God guard our hearts and minds.

You give us the grace not to worry about tomorrow, and deal with each challenge that comes our way, one day at a time.

Lord, we're praying for peace. We're praying for provision.

Lord, we steep our life in the God reality, the God initiative, and the God provision.

As we do, I speak a blessing that we're not missing out. Lord, as we put you first and give our entire attention to you and say, God, help our family, help our friends, help our work. Help our business, Lord, take care of us, as we put you first.

We don't have to get worked up, frustrated, angry, and anxious.

When things don't work out, we can trust you.

We give you the attention to say: you're first in our lives. And as we do, we don't have to seek the temporal things. You can bless us.

Thank you, Lord. Amen.

IN CONCLUSION

Father, you are the Eternal One, the Alpha and Omega, the first in the last, the beginning and the end. You know our situations and circumstances. You're going to take care of us.

You know the sorrow, the pain, the heartache, and we give them to you.

You know the joys, the celebrations, the thrills, the wonder. Thank you. We worship and adore you.

Bless us indeed.

Amen!

ABOUT THE AUTHORS

Bob Perry, a self-described "fasting intercessor," has been a student of prayer for four decades. He constantly seeks to hone his craft, studying not only how people pray around the globe and throughout history, but also constantly asking, "Lord, teach me to pray." He lives in East Nashville, Tennessee with his wife, and enjoys spending time with his four adult children.

He has led multiple prayer initiatives that have trained and mobilized hundreds of thousands of people in prayer. An author and coach, currently he serves the business community, praying for business owners in every sphere of influence.

Find him at workplaceprayer.com.

***

Amy Lykosh is an author, mentor, and entrepreneur. Through Workplace Prayer, Makarios Press, the Make Prayer Beautiful podcast, and more, she covers businesses in prayer and raises up intercessors to do the same. She lives outside Charlottesville, Virginia with her husband and five sons.

Enjoy the Prayer Refresh: 21 short prayers to pray as you go about your day. praybig.me/refresh

Made in the USA
Middletown, DE
26 September 2024